BROKEN VESSELS, GOLDEN LIGHT

A Prayer for the Broken

Nyah Seraphine

SERAPHINE
HOUSE PRESS

Title: Broken Vessels, Golden Light

Subtitle: A Prayer for the Broken

Author: Nyah Seraphine

First edition: 2026

ISBN (paperback): 979-8-9946572-0-1

Scripture quotations taken from The Holy Bible, New International Version® NIV®
Copyright © 1973, 1978, 1984, 2011 by Biblica, Inc.
Used with permission. All rights reserved worldwide.

Cover art and design: [Nyah Seraphine/ CANVA]

Interior design: Nyah Seraphine

Printed in the United States of America.

For information, contact: nyahseraphinewrites@gmail.com

Disclaimer:

This book is a work of art and personal expression. Names, identifying details, and certain elements may have been changed to protect privacy. The experiences and emotions depicted are presented through the lens of poetry and are not intended to represent factual statements about any specific individual. This book is not medical, legal, or psychological advice.

"But we have this treasure in jars of clay to show that this all-surpassing power is from God and not from us."

2 Corinthians 4:7 (NIV)

Preface

This book is not a performance of strength.
It is a hymn from the places where I cracked - and did not disappear.

I have carried questions in my body the way some people carry weather:
Will I be loved without shrinking?

Will God meet me in the rooms I keep locked?
Can a woman be bruised and still be blessed?

These poems were written across years and seasons - girlhood, womanhood, and the long holy work between.

Some were born in midnight ache. Some arrived at dawn like mercy.
All of them are witnesses.

If you have ever learned to smile while your spirit was aching,
if you have ever mistaken survival for love,
if you have ever buried the child within you just to keep going - come close.

Read slowly, like prayer.
Take what nourishes you, leave what is not yours, and let the light be gentle.
May these pages be a place where the broken are not shamed, only gathered.

I spent years mistaking longing for love. I searched for it in parents who could not give what they did not carry, and in men who offered the shape of love without the substance of it. I learned the ache of waiting, the fatigue of proving, the quiet grief of being almost chosen.

These poems are the record of that schooling - and the holy turn that followed. When human love would not hold, I began to gather myself. I began to mother myself. I began to trust that God's love is not a performance, but a covering. And little by little, I learned: the truest love is the one that returns you to yourself - and to Him.

Dedication

To the child within me -
and to the child within you -

To every woman who learned to be brave too early,
and every soul who kept breathing anyway.

To my ancestors,
whose prayers still travel through my blood.

And to God,
who meets us in the cracks
and calls that place holy.

CONTENTS

Preface

Dedication

Part I - The Girl Inside the Woman

LOVE

1978 - age 11

I wrote this after watching my mother love my father and watching him refuse her in return. What I saw didn't feel like love - it felt like performance. This poem is the beginning of my skepticism.

Love is unreal.

Love is a pretense.

Love is what you think you feel.

Love makes no sense.

Mothering the Child Within

June 12, 2015 (around 5:00 AM) - age 47
I wrote this as a homecoming. I stopped burying the child inside me and
brought her forward - into safety, into God, into my own arms. This is the
moment love became something I could mother, not chase.

I envelop her fragile body in my mothering arms.
I know now that by trying to bury her deeply within,
I too had abandoned her, left her alone and unable to mend.

She'd starved so long for love sought from earthly molds.
Not knowing that her heavenly Father had it all under His
control.

She curled up inside of me in the cavern of my soul
And protected something beautiful, bruised, and battered.
She held it close to secure it lest further damage be bestowed.

I bring her forward now. I open my heart where I had her
encased within.
Now a mother myself, I mother myself.

I mother myself to peace.
I mother myself to courage.
I mother myself to strength.
I mother myself to forgiveness.
I mother myself to trust.
I mother myself to joy.
I mother myself to love.
I mother myself to renewal.
I mother myself to rebirth.

By joining us, I am transformed.
I am whole. I am powerful. I am loved.
I.
Am.
LOVE.

3

Not Enough

Feb. 6, 2016 - age 48

I wrote this as a meeting between the woman I became and the child I once was. It is my testimony about what a lack of tenderness can do - and what it means to finally choose myself.

To the little girl with beautiful eyes who resides within my soul,

I know what "Not Enough" has done to you,

I know dearth's wicked toll.

When love did not cover you in January like a warm blanket in wintry bliss,

You surrounded us with paper parents who didn't belittle, beat, or dismiss.

But paper is thin and stiff, and the imagination - a poor substitute for a hug -

That's when we learned to pretend we didn't care and mastered the mean mug.

In April, when sapling leaves began to bud with the beauty and brilliance of Spring,

We heard not enough of true value and worth, too much of "you're ugly" and "vain".

So, we began to avoid mirrors, including even the reflections in others' eyes.

We began to absorb the poison and graduated from self-doubt to self-despise.

Like a butterfly we flitted from flower to flower, seeking that one elusive thing.

But, instead of the sweet nectar we sought, we received abuse's bitter sting.

Doubly wounded as we were by the slings and arrows of life's defeat,

We deliberately cut our losses, settling for a nice guy who didn't beat.

But by June we were tired of playing the roles of both husband AND wife,

So we decided we would be much better off alone, free from marital strife.

For what good is being married, when one's 'partner' has long been outgrown?

'Twas no good being yoked with one, who - when together - felt like being alone.

Dearth, we are done with you. Begone! We're reaching now for what is ours!

We deserve the best from life and no longer accept your colorless, icy towers.

We join together she and I, and become one now. I know Abundance is what I'll find,

For Dearth, you are simply Not Enough for me - I'm too good for what you have in mind!

My Winter Dreams

1980 - age 13

I wrote this during a season when my inner world felt cold and crowded with shadows. Even then, I could name the ache - and I could translate it into weather.

My Winter Dreams are Snowy Folds

Where shadows lurk and hearts are cold.

In frigid caves encased in ice,

My winter dreams are not so nice.

Bathed in darkness, damp and smooth,

My winter dreams do not soothe.

Broken promises and tarnished dreams,

Flowless rivers and frozen streams,

These are found in my winter dreams.

With aching soul quivering in pain,

And broken heart I try to feign

Happiness as slowly I go insane.

In my winter dreams, the birds don't sing,

And heart over mind always reigns.

The Graduate

July 3, 1990 - age 22
This poem stands at the threshold between outward achievement and inward fear - naming the quiet truth behind the gown.

As I looked into the mirror that morning, I saw a
Woman standing firm and tall at the threshold of life.
My eyes had a certain gleam in them, my graduation gown
became my complexion.
.

I looked prepared to succeed at anything I set my mind to do.
My reflection shone with confidence.

The mirror lied.

Behind that mask of confidence hid a child-woman
Small, scared and alone, teetering on the threshold of life;
Trying with uncertainty to get a foothold on the future.
The gleam in my eyes was caused by light reflecting
on tears of frustration, sorrow and self-pity.

My graduation gown deftly hid my un-ironed dress,
Which I had quickly donned, having overslept once again.
I was prepared to forego graduation exercises, fearing that my
name wouldn't be called and I'd have to face a sea of shame.

At last, my name is announced, and I walk up to
the stage to accept the empty diploma container.
As I glide away, a mass of carefully concealed nerves,
I can't help but feel as if I am stepping blindly off a path
And onto a tightrope, where each step could lead to doom.

Puzzle

Dec. 15, 1990 - age 23

I wrote this while learning that a person can be many selves at once: the self we show, the self we hide, and the self we are still becoming. This poem is a mirror that doesn't flatter - it tells the truth.

I see fragmented pieces of myself everywhere.

Disembodied shadows written in ink on the

pages of some story or another echo ME.

In the laughing face of a small child, or in

the wearied eyes of an elderly woman.

Who I am I have yet to discover.

Sometimes, I see myself through the eyes of

another self – yet unknown to me, and I am frightened.

Me the current, now laughing at some inane joke

or at some hopeless situation that I have once

again brought upon myself. Now sober and sad,

pondering the complexities of life. Displaying

to all the world only the mirrored images of what

it wants or thinks it sees; while the other ME

silently watches, waiting patiently for the moment when the

fragments will be pulled together like so many pieces of a puzzle.

Pain

May 22, 2014 — age 46
I wrote this as a plain-spoken truth: pain had become familiar, like a home I never chose. This poem names the tangled threads —and the fear that I might never break free from it.

Pain,

Carried in my body like a turtle does its shell,

Has always been my 'home', my personal living hell.

From childhood to womanhood, one pain has led to more.

Each thread that binds a spider silk grown too dense to shore.[1]

[1] *shore: archaic past tense of shear; used by Shakespeare (e.g., A Midsummer Night's Dream 5.1).*

Interlude I - The Door

I did not arrive here whole.
I arrived here breathing.

If you are reading this,
you have crawled through something, too.

Come in -
not to be impressed,
not to be repaired like a broken chair,
but to be held like a living thing.

We will name the ache
without worshiping it.
We will tell the truth
without turning it into a tomb.

And if you tremble,
that is only your spirit
remembering
it still has feeling.

Interlude II - Letter to the Little One

Little girl,
I know you learned silence early.

I know you tried to be easy to love -
small enough to keep,
bright enough to deserve.

But you do not have to earn tenderness.
You are not a chore.
You are not a problem.

If no one taught you how to be held,
let me teach you now:

Come closer.
Rest here.
You are safe with me.

Part II - The Ways We Break

Free
1989 - age 22
I wrote this as a goodbye without bargaining. It is the moment I understood that love cannot be forced - and survival sometimes looks like letting go with dignity.

So I set you free, hoping,

As the poem goes, that if

You really loved me,

You would return.

Well, you haven't returned

And I have my answer.

I love you. Have a nice life.

No. Don't worry about me.

I will survive - barely.

Love Tree

1988 - age 21

I wrote this after a love was cut down, not gently ended. This poem is what it sounds like when innocence realizes it has been used - and refuses to pretend it can grow back unchanged.

Once a tree is cut, its stump never regains the splendor and

Magnificence it enjoyed as a tree. It is simply a plain old

Useless tree stump.

You viciously cut down our love, and I watched its

Beauty wither up and die like a flower

Which has been plucked to adorn, only momentarily, a vase on
the table.

My love, sacrificed to satisfy your own primitive needs,

Will never again reach the dizzying heights it achieved in its
innocence.

Eclipse

2002 - age 35

I wrote this as a warning to myself and to women: don't shrink into orbit.
Some love asks you to dim so someone else can shine - and that is not love, it
is erasure.

Men.

I swear the world has yet to create

one that is right for me.

When it comes to the subject of men,

Chile, I have a past that is less than forgettable

And a future that is unforeseeable.

You see, my life has been riddled with

Mistakes and all of them men.

I don't know why I even bother with them.

We are as different from them as the moon is from the sun.

We 'revolve' around them.

Billions of miles away, we watch as they light the

heavens with their male egos, then

grudgingly allow us the briefest of moments

to cast our own subtler light across the skies,

Only to slip quietly away before 'his majesty' makes an

appearance.

Seldom do we deny him his right to sit

Upon the throne,

 and then of course you see where

That leads us

--- into total darkness!

There are Times

June 1989 - age 21

*This poem circles the ache of longing that returns in waves - waking,
searching, resisting, and dreaming again.*

There are times when,
During the dawn of my awakening
(when reality is poised just upon the edge of a dream),
I long for you. My fingers reach out, but alas, to touch only
The cool, lonely spot where you used to be, long, long ago.

There are times when, during the morning
Hours of my awareness,
I find myself looking for you everywhere:
In every voice, I hear your voice. Calling me.
Playing with my emotions once again.

There are times when, my senses dulled by the activities
Of the day, I am tired of anticipation, and want only to
Rest and forget about the bitter after-taste
Of a love gone sour.

There are times when, as night approaches,
I try not to succumb to fatigue…
Knowing that sleep will only bring dreams…
And dreams will only lead me back to you.

For, you see, only in my dreams does our love remain.
Every night our kisses enflame my love for you…
But suddenly, the dream ends.
I awaken,

And I am doomed to dream again.

I Will Not Fight for You

Feb. 18, 2020 - age 52

I wrote this as a boundary and a vow. I was naming a kind of disrespect that tries to turn a woman into a contestant - and I refused the game.

"So, where should I sit?" she smirked as she sat right down next to you.

She laughed -

And those boys, they covered stretched mouths behind their hands and they grinned too.

For they knew that you'd been betwixt her thighs, once upon a time, and now mine are the ones that draw you.

I felt it rend and break a bit, this thing I have for you.

You seem to take joy in seeing leftover, discarded vessels all about you – do you glory in the idea that all who know you can see the mess of used-to-be's mixed with the new?

Maybe you expect me to fight for you?

That... I would never do.

I do not fight for what should have been mine all along, and I will not fight for you.

One of Us

July 15, 2018 - age 51

I wrote this as a burial and a boundary. It is for the version of me who tried to survive on promises - and the version of me who finally chose herself.

He came back to find her. She of the soft heart and hands.

She who had believed in his lies, and sweet words. She, who had clung to them and to him as if they were her lifeline.

But she died long ago. Ripped, shredded, bleeding out and buried up to her head in the mud of men's deceit.

You see, one of us had to go.

And she, being the giving and sensitive one - chose to fall on the sword.

A martyr so that one of us could live.

So, you see, you won't find her here.

She is gone.

She died without a whimper.

Things

April 30, 1993 - age 25

This poem captures the chilling quiet of a love ending - when even your grief is met with indifference.

I told him I intended to leave him.
He changed the channel on the t.v.

Silence.

I could not breathe, the lump in my throat grew
As the pain in my heart intensified.

Last to so many things.

Letting Go

2008 - age 41

I wrote this when I realized that holding on can be a slow form of self-abandonment. This is not a bitter release - it is a loving one: for them, and for me.

Some people think it's holding on that makes one strong –

But sometimes it's letting go.

I let you go. Not because I don't love you anymore,

But because you need to be strong. And you can only do this without me, and by standing

On your own feet.

I am letting you go because I cannot continue to watch us tear each other apart. I can't continue

To expect more for you than you do for your own self.

I'm letting you go because I want you to find someone whom you can

Truly love passionately with your WHOLE heart.

I'm letting you go so that you can learn to believe in yourself.

So that you can begin to motivate yourself and discover and

Achieve your own dreams.

I'm letting you go so that we might both re-discover our own wonderful, individual selves.

I'm letting you go because we are like two unevenly yoked beasts.

I pull and pull, dragging you along against your will. You resent that. I resent that.

I'm letting you go because I love you. But most of all, I'm letting you go because I love me.

If we can't bring each other joy, let's at least not bring each other pain.

Return of the Muse

1993 - age 25–26

*This poem marks the moment the voice returns: the muse insists on truth,
and healing begins even when you resist it.*

The Muse returned months ago, but I ignored it – hoping that if I
didn't write the 'healing' poem, I wouldn't need to heal.

I was fooling myself.
The healing started months ago.
Months of tears and frustration with a relationship already
souring.

I tried to hang on, thinking "I can't let this relationship fail".
But, subconsciously, I knew.
I knew it had failed already.
That it had never really had a chance.

Love isn't lasting when one gives more than the other.
As I see it, you defaulted on a loan and now, shamed
By my own naiveté, I am taking my heart back.

You never asked for it anyway.

Interlude III - Rules I Don't Break Myself With

I will not chase what refuses me.
I will not beg for a seat
at a table that feeds me scraps.

I will not confuse intensity with intimacy,
or attention with love.

I will not compete with ghosts
for a man's shaky ego.

I will not call chaos "chemistry."
Not anymore.

I will choose peace -
even when peace is lonely at first.

Interlude IV - The Body Remembers

My body is not dramatic.
It is precise.

It remembers what my mouth swallowed.
It remembers the nights I smiled anyway.
It remembers the weight of being unseen.

Some mornings I wake up tired
and mistake it for weakness.

But no -
I am simply carrying history
in muscle and marrow,
in breath and blood.

So I listen now.
I ask:
What are you trying to tell me
that I refused to hear?

Part III - When the World Hurts

Roots/Culture/Life

January 30, 1993 - age 25

*This poem is an ancestral meditation—growth pulling you away from the
roots that fed you, and the reverent return to heritage as soil, anchor, and
strength.*

The seed
becomes the sapling;
the sapling becomes the tree.
The higher the sapling grows,
the further from roots it be.

I - like the sapling - grew up to be the tree.
The older I become, the farther my roots they be.
The distance - due to growth - much wider in mentality.

Did the same roots that fed the sapling, also nourish the tree?
I ask myself this question, and always the answer – it be:
The tree once was the sapling, the sapling once the seed, but
without roots
to ground firmly in soil, nothing would they be.

Almost at once I realize the soil to be my past –
rich in Black-American culture, a strong and healthy repast.
The roots to be my heritage, anchoring me quick and fast.
The trunk to be my family providing
strength and support to last.

Humbly, I acknowledge – why... I'm not a tree at all,
but merely a small shoot, a tiny little thing –
still green and tender with inexperience, still in the throes of
spring

Where growth's sometimes so painful that many cannot cling
Give up and fall
back
down
to

earth
to be reborn again.

I, like the
tiny shoot,
still yearning to be the tree,
resign myself to the fact
- a limb's the most I'll be.
Part of the whole but not the entirety.

O' Tree wonderful tree, how I envy thee!
Ancient as the times, what all did you see?
Were you a seed when time began?
A sapling when you first saw man?
Do your roots stretch to the ends of the earth?
Did you bear witness to civilization's birth?
O' Tree wonderful tree,
How I wish I were thee.

400 Years

Apr. 1990 - age 22

I wrote this from the ache of inheritance - the kind of grief that isn't only personal, but historical. This poem is a question I needed to ask out loud: where do we belong, after so much has been taken?

400 years we've been here

And still no peace of mind.

400 years we've been here

Still we don't belong.

400 years we've been away

And still no call from home.

400 years we've been away.

We no longer belong.

400 years and still we struggle

To belong to someone, some thing.

Here, they don't want us because

We don't fit their 'all-American' mold.

There, they don't want us because

We're not REALLY one of them at all.

We just don't fit that 'African' mold.

MOTHER Africa, is this how you welcome
Back your own lost children?

400 years, and America, you still can't accept us
As your very own.

We, who have bled, toiled and died for you.

Black Americans what shall we do?

Our 'fellow' Americans and our African 'cousins' have
abandoned us.

MY brothers, MY sisters, what shall we do?

Sometimes, I do believe that we are amongst

The most unwanted people of all.

Children of Darkness

July 3, 1990 - age 22

I wrote this as a call for awakening. It speaks to the darkness that lives in human behavior - and to the possibility of choosing light, together.

We are children of the dark,

We are children of darkness,

We are dark children:

White, Black, Brown, Yellow, and Red - we are ALL children of darkness.

Come forth into the light of understanding, peace and brotherly love.

We must free our minds from their oppression,

We must free ourselves from hatred, distrust and fear that

Has dimmed the light in our hearts.

Children of darkness come walk hand in hand with me

Out into the light of love and trust.

We shall learn how to honor one another

And slowly, we shall begin to love again.

Can't Stop Crying and Praying

May 2010 - age 42

I wrote this as lament and witness. When the world kept hurting children and calling it "normal," I couldn't numb myself - so I cried, I prayed, and I wrote.

Can't stop crying:
For a 14-year-old boy who lost his life in a haze of bullets as he played basketball with a friend on the eve of Mother's Day. A talented, smart child who looked forward to a promising life, he never saw the end coming. All his hopes, dreams and aspirations – gone in the blink of an eye, leaving a family and community shattered. I pray for his soul.

Can't stop crying:
For a 14-year-old whose warm lifeblood ebbed out onto a frozen sidewalk one cold afternoon in February. I pray for his soul. Gunned down in broad daylight on a busy highway yet no one saw a thing – their eyes and ears deliberately shut to the horrors and evil around them. Adults in the neighborhood console themselves by saying 'there must have been more to that than meets the eye'. As if that somehow justified the fact that someone took the life of this child. We falsely believe that our own children are somehow safe because surely bullets have names written on them, don't they? Wrong. I pray for our souls.

I pray for all children who are slain, cut down as seedlings. May the Lord hold their precious souls safe in His arms -- may they finally know peace.

Can't stop crying:
For three young boys who committed suicide after being bullied relentlessly at school -
Two 11-year-olds tormented by the malicious unthinking taunts of other children who called them 'faggot', 'gay' and racist slurs – couldn't survive in the brutal atmosphere of hatred and intolerance. I pray for their souls.

For a 13-year-old tormented and bullied for years because of his small size. Too young to realize that at his age, small stature is temporary, but death permanent. I pray for his soul.

Can't stop crying:
For an 8-year-old who attempted to kill himself by jumping out a 2nd floor window at his school after being persistently bullied by other children because he has dyslexia. I pray for his soul.

For a 13-year-old girl tormented and bullied into committing suicide by boys and girls at her school. Wanting to fit in, trying to be cool, she'd engaged in sexting - sending nude pictures of herself to a boy. She strangled herself in her bedroom while her parents were downstairs cooking dinner. She said she couldn't take the pain anymore. I pray for her soul.

For a 15-year-old girl who took her own life after being maliciously harassed, maligned and tormented by bullies. She'd been in the US only months before her tormentors pushed her into taking her own life. Having reached out for help and having been thwarted at each turn, the pain and torture became too much for her young soul to take. Upon learning of her suicide, one young bully wrote "mission accomplished." I pray for her soul.

Cry for all children – both young and old. Pray for us all.

The children who took their own lives knew not what they were doing. They simply wanted to stop the pain. Adults, who were supposed to be caring for them, protecting them, failed them. They were tender shoots choked by the bitter weeds of life. Their young spirits overburdened - heavy with grief, laden with pain. Shed tears for them. Pray for them.

Shed tears for the souls of child bullies and child murderers - so young yet so malevolent. Too soon they have become the monsters, the killers of innocence – not only of others but of their own. May they obtain forgiveness. May they find the mercy that they themselves denied their victims. I pray for their souls.

Shed tears for those of us who bear witness. Those of us who daily turn a blind eye, a deaf ear, a closed mouth to the pain and torment of others, for we are all children of God and all life is invaluable. Pray for us all.

Mourn those of us who speak with forked tongues that condemn, maim, and destroy. Weep for those of us who see through eyes too quick to notice small differences yet too slow to recognize vast similarities. Pray for us all.

Grieve for those of us with small and petty minds that cannot grasp this truth -- when we judge others, we in fact judge ourselves. Pray for us all.

Will our most lasting legacy be the teaching of intolerance to our children? Will we continue to damage and destroy young minds and souls by training them in hatred, bigotry, depravity, and cruelty?

LORD JESUS, I PRAY WE WAKE UP! PURGE OUR HEARTS. CHANGE THE PATH WE ARE ON. WE MUST FIGHT TO SAVE OUR HUMANITY, SAVE OUR BABIES, SAVE OUR WORLD. TO SAVE OUR VERY SOULS!

How do we turn back from this abyss? Death is all around us and I just can't stop crying and praying.

Interlude V - When the World Hurts

Some pain is personal.
Some pain is inherited.

Some grief is mine.
Some grief is a river
running through generations.

When I cry for the child on the news,
for the mother who keeps burying hope,
for the hard-faced man who learned cruelty -
I am not weak.

I am awake.

And I will not numb myself
to survive a world
that needs healing.

I will stay tender,
and let tenderness
be my protest.

Part IV - The Gold

"Those who cleanse themselves from the latter will be instruments for special purposes, made holy, useful to the Master and prepared to do any good work."
- 2 Timothy 2:21 (NIV)

The Shallow End: a warning

May 22, 2014 (around 2:00 AM) - age 46
A threshold warning: feel the sorrow, listen to the soul, but do not let grief become an abyss that seduces you to drown.

Wade into the shallow end of sorrow.

Sit a while in soul's despair and indulge in the sound
Of spirit' cries.

But dive ye not too deep into this Abyss
of wretchedness.

For there, Sirens lure souls to drown where Ka* dies.

*Ka: in ancient Egyptian belief, the life-force (spirit) of a person.

Burmese Ruby (Vow)

January 17, 2026 (morning) - age 58
The woman I used to be did not recognize her worth. She offered her holy
trinity—mind, body, and spirit—to men who never earned her. The woman
I am becoming knows her value and will not share her energy with anyone
who cannot truly see her.

The next time, my precious heart,
the ones who hold you
will have earned their place
in your chambers—

for they will know you
for the rarest gift that you are,
more precious
than a Burmese ruby.

For my mind—
do not come to me
with tangled tongues,
with circles dressed up as truth,
with "depth" that is only fog.

I have lived too long
inside confusion
to invite it back in
and call it love.

Speak plain.
Speak clean.
or
do not speak to me
at all.

For my body—
do not reach for me
with borrowed tenderness,
with hunger that has no honor,
with hands that take

what they have not earned.

My body is not proof.
Not payment.
Not a place
to unload your emptiness.

Come with reverence—
or
don't come.

For my soul—
that chamber is not yours.
It never was.

It is God's.
Sealed.
Kept.
Covered
in golden light.

And I will not trade
what is holy
for what is temporary.

So yes—
the next time my heart opens,
it will open for hands
that know
what they are holding.

I know my worth.
I know my power.

I recognize myself—
rare...
and precious.

And I will not suffer fools again.

I will not
dim
again.

Broken

June 3, 2018 - age 50

I wrote this in a season when I felt tired of carrying my own heart. This poem is what happened when light interrupted me - not to blame me nor shame me, but to remind me that trying is no sin.

Erupting through darkness, Light cast its ill-timed glare,

It whispered "Get up. Trying is no sin."

As I lay crumpled at the bottom of the stair.

I, so annoyed by the soul child within,

Complained "Why? I will just fall again!"

"These stairs are crooked, you see how they bend!"

Laden with dreams of love unfulfilled, I had fallen and fractured.

Why am I so broken?

Broken Vessels

July 5, 2018 (rev. Feb. 2019) - age 51
I wrote this as a refusal to believe that breaking makes us worthless. This is
my declaration that love can pour through cracks - and that healing can
make a vessel luminous.

Who will love a broken woman like me?

A man who is true, would love me scars and all.

A man who sought to build something indestructible

would join his broken self with my broken self –

for although I am broken, I am strong.

How could I not be? I, who was starved of love, yet do have a
bottomless capacity to give it -- for the source of my love is
something that cannot be - emptied.

Although I am broken, cracked, scarred and battered, I am brave
and fiercely hopeful. I will open up this heart of mine and pour
out my love again, and again, and again, and again -- until I am no
more.

Love flows unfettered through the cracks of broken vessels.

———————————

In some ways, we are all like broken vessels. Psalm 31:12 KJV "I
am forgotten as a dead man out of mind; I am like a broken
vessel." But, as we know, God finds purpose, yes -- even for
broken vessels, for it is sometimes through our cracks that His
light shines through.

Step On

2003 - age 35

*This is a courage-vow in miniature—movement as medicine, choosing one
step over paralysis, even with the risk of falling.*

I must step,
I must step,
I must make my first step somewhere.
Even if it is into a hole, I must step.
I can no longer remain motionless, rooted in terror.
Too overcome with the fear of failing.
Step on. I must.
Even if I may fall

From Whence Cometh My Love

Sept. 3, 2014 - age 47

I wrote this as a reminder that love is not only something we receive - it is also a source inside us. This is the sound of my spirit claiming its own well.

From whence cometh my love?

From that place deep within which cannot be bound

From that concert of my heart blazing with sound

From outside the edge of that which can't be found

From my soul in its perfection - whole and round

From whence cometh my love?

It's from heaven above!

Come Shepherd My Love
1982 - age 15

*I wrote this as a vow for the kind of love I wanted - steady, tender, and
lasting. Even at fifteen and having never been kissed, I knew I didn't want
performance; I wanted shelter. I wrote it in response (albeit a 20th century
one) to 16th century poet Christopher Marlowe's poem, The Passionate
Shepherd to His Love.*

I will come to thee, and be thy love
And we shall all our pleasures prove.

But you must know that dells and hills
Lakes and rivers to time soon yield.

Likewise, beauty of form and face,
As water erodes rock, time soon shall erase.

Pleasures of body are easily taken,
But pleasures of the soul cannot be forsaken.

Expensive dresses, shoes, and velvet capes
As years pass by, doth lose their shapes.

Luxury cars, jewelry and fancy trips
Cannot compare to thine companionship.

Lust and desire are quenched as time quells the fire
But true love, tenderness and affection doth never expire.

If you promise to dance with me in the rain
And love the same once age my face doth stain.

Come December-evening with its gray, cold mist
I'll be wrapped in your arms, still warmed with bliss.

Come Shepherd, promise me I will always be your dove,
and I will come live with thee and be thy one true love.

Sisters

October 7, 1990 - age 23
*This is a letter-poem of belonging—sisterhood as shared soul, mutual
freedom, and lifelong shelter.*

Jennifer,
Wherever this life may lead me and whatever things I do
Please always do remember that I'm a part of you.
Inextricably bound together are we, like two halves of a whole –
Two people in two bodies but possessing a single soul.

So love yourself dearly, and forever strive to be free
For remember my dear sister that you're also a part of me.
And one day I hope to be able, as a loving sign,
To enrich your life as half as much as you have enriched mine.
I will love you always, dearest sister.

Interlude VI - A Prayer for the Broken

God of the cracked places,
meet me where I split.

Not with punishment.
Not with shame.
With light that doesn't burn.

Gather the pieces I dropped
while trying to be strong.

Teach me the courage
of soft living,
of honest no's,
of clean goodbyes.

Fill the fractures with gold
until even my scars confess:
I lived.
I loved.
I learned.
I returned.

Interlude VII - Benediction: Golden Light

May your healing be quiet and real,
and need no permission.

May you stop calling yourself "too much"
for people who offered too little.

May love come like clean water -
not as a bargain,
not as a trap.

And when you feel broken,
may you remember:

A vessel can crack
and still carry light.

Legacy Blessing

In the words of my late grandma, C. Louise, who died reciting Psalm 121 (I Lift My Eyes To The Hills):

I AM BLESSED—BETTER THAN BLESSED.
EVEN HERE, EVEN NOW, GOD IS KEEPING ME.

Reader Affirmations
(for closure and becoming)

I AM NO LONGER AVAILABLE FOR
RELATIONSHIPS THAT DIMINISH
MY LIGHT, DISTORT MY TRUTH, OR
DISHONOR MY LOVE.

I SPEAK MY TRUTH WITHOUT
SHAME, AND I CHOOSE PEACE
WITHOUT PERMISSION.

I AM WORTHY OF SAFE,
RESPECTFUL, AND RECIPROCAL
LOVE.

I RELEASE THE PAST WITH
GRATITUDE FOR ITS LESSONS.

I WALK FORWARD IN
WHOLENESS AND FREEDOM.

GOD MEETS ME IN MY BROKEN PLACES
AND FILLS ME WITH GOLDEN LIGHT.

I DO NOT DIM AGAIN.

Becoming Me

I am allowed to be free.

I am allowed to release what once
helped me survive.

I am allowed to step into the next
chapter - not with fear, but with authority...

Not with shame, but with reverence for
all I've overcome...

For all I am
and all that I am becoming.

Beginning
April 2025

When the relationship I believed would be my happy ending came to a close, I felt a door shut—and another open. This poem is a prayer for beginnings: for the love that grows inward, for the purpose that waits patiently, and for the peace that arrived when I finally chose myself.

Maybe the happy ending
isn't an ending at all -
but a beginning,
where I fall in love with my own life.

Where I awaken in a land far from
sorrow,
breathe in peace,
and write the books that have waited
patiently inside my bones.

Where I taste joy on my tongue,
chase sunrises across unfamiliar skies,
read pages that mirror my becoming,
and dance barefoot beneath the moon.

Where I live gently -
fully, freely,
with calm in my soul
and fire in my spirit.

And maybe, just maybe,
the truest love story
is the one I write
between me and myself -
whole, unconditional,
and overflowing into the lives
of those ready to receive it.

About the Author

Nyah Seraphine (pseudonym) is a writer whose work explores love, grief, spiritual transformation, and the quiet bravery of becoming whole. Her poetry is rooted in truth-telling and the belief that healing is both personal and sacred. *Broken Vessels, Golden Light: A Prayer for the Broken* is her debut collection, and she is currently working to finalize her first novel.

Nyah is a healer. An allied health professional by vocation and by calling. She entered the healing arts after learning, earlier in life, that we are far more connected than we can see—by grief, by love, by spirit, and by what we carry in our bodies. In tending to others, she discovered a holy mystery: that helping to facilitate healing in someone else sometimes stimulates one's own healing. Her work in the healing industry continues to shape her writing, where broken places are not rejected, but met—gently—and filled with golden light.

www.ingramcontent.com/pod-product-compliance
Lightning Source LLC
Chambersburg PA
CBHW051646120626
46551CB00015B/2245